resonant eyes

I0485599

a coloring book of mandalas, mandorlas, and

geometry by

Anji Marth

this book is dedicated to all fjl's,

oddballs,

and cat enthusiasts I have known.

section one:

full-page mandalas and

mandorlas

When I was very young, I drew freely, without fear.

I colored as well as I could, but also without anxiety.

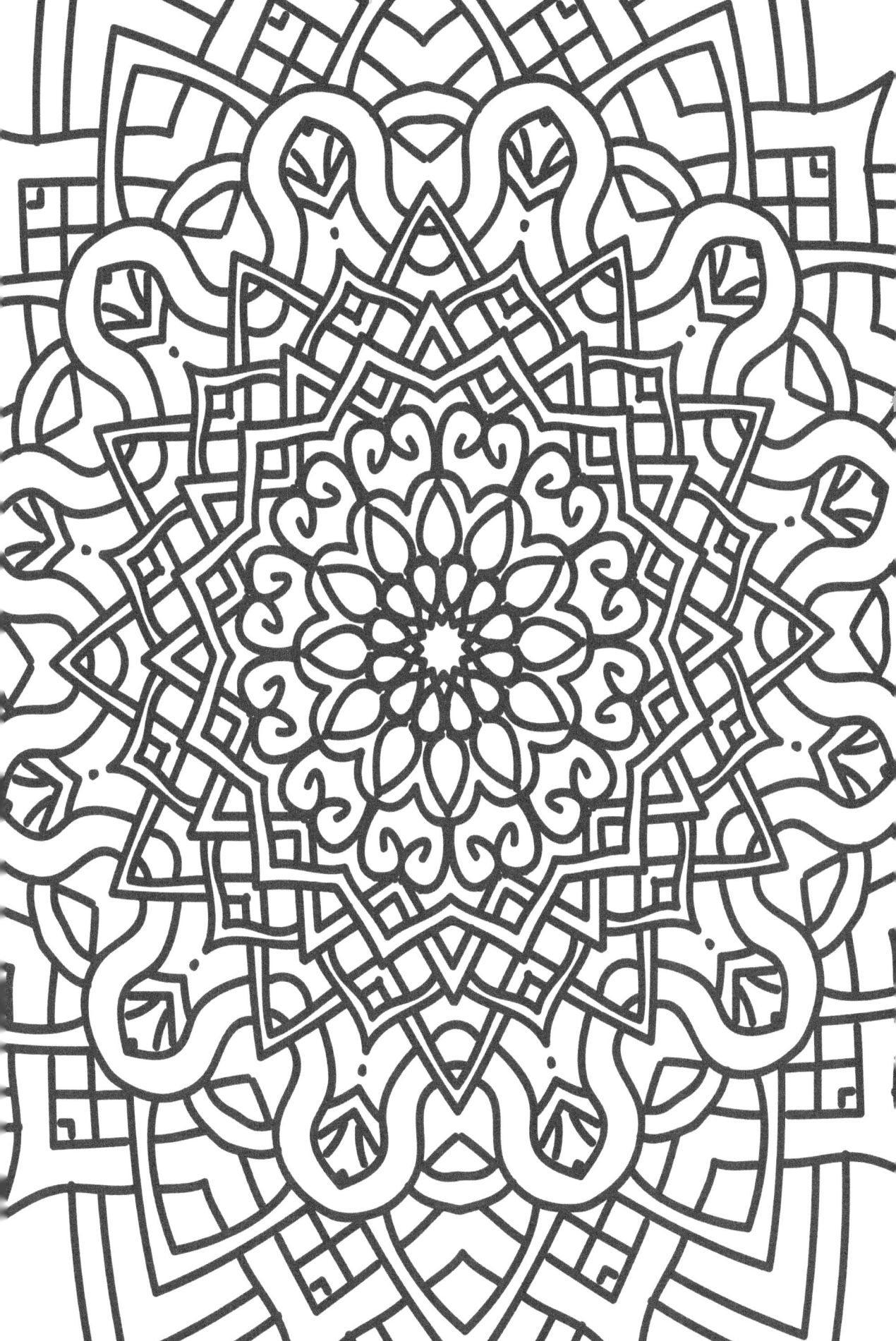

I knew that the results mattered much less than the act of putting pen or crayon to paper.

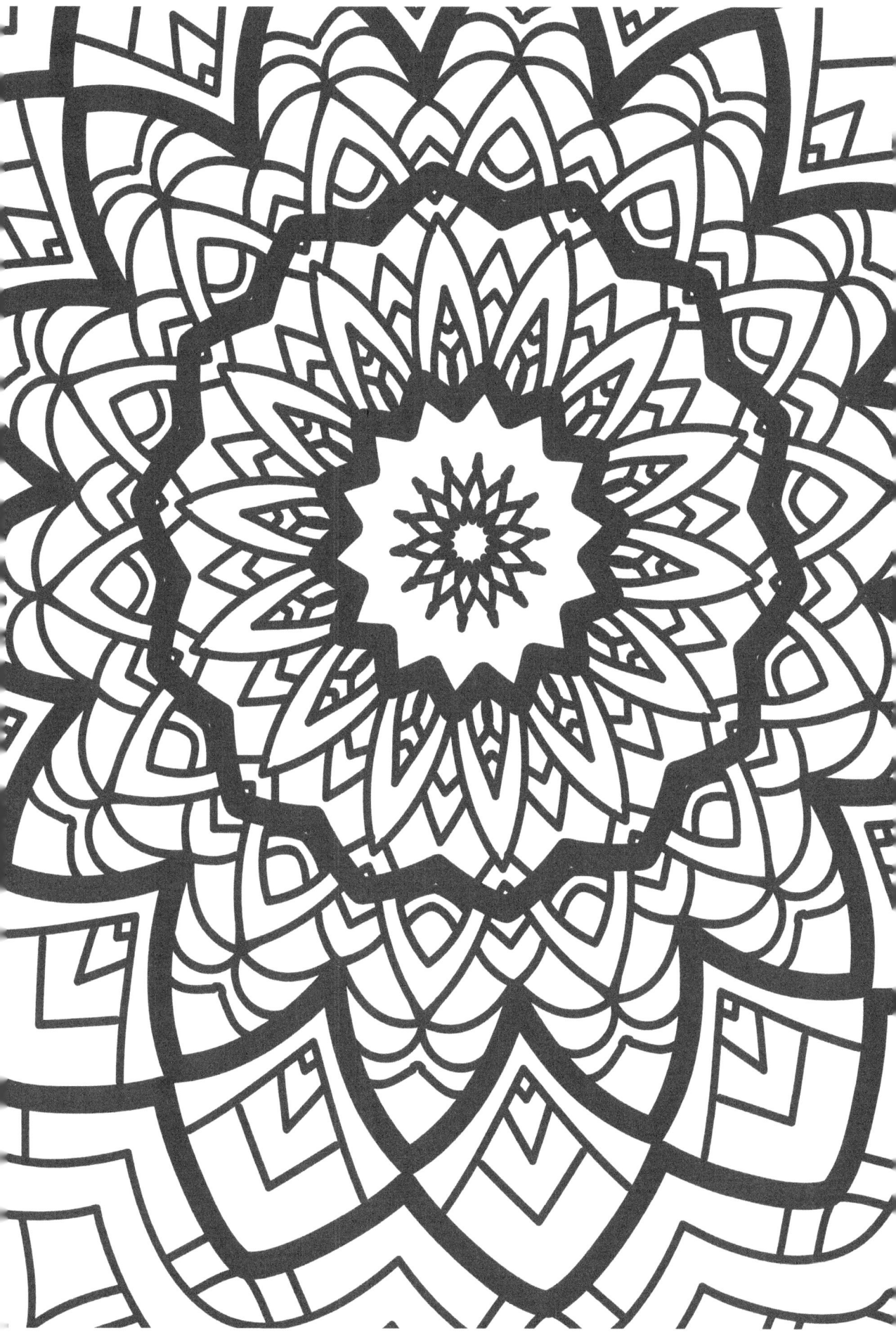

When you're coloring,
you can't make any
mistakes.

It's not a test.

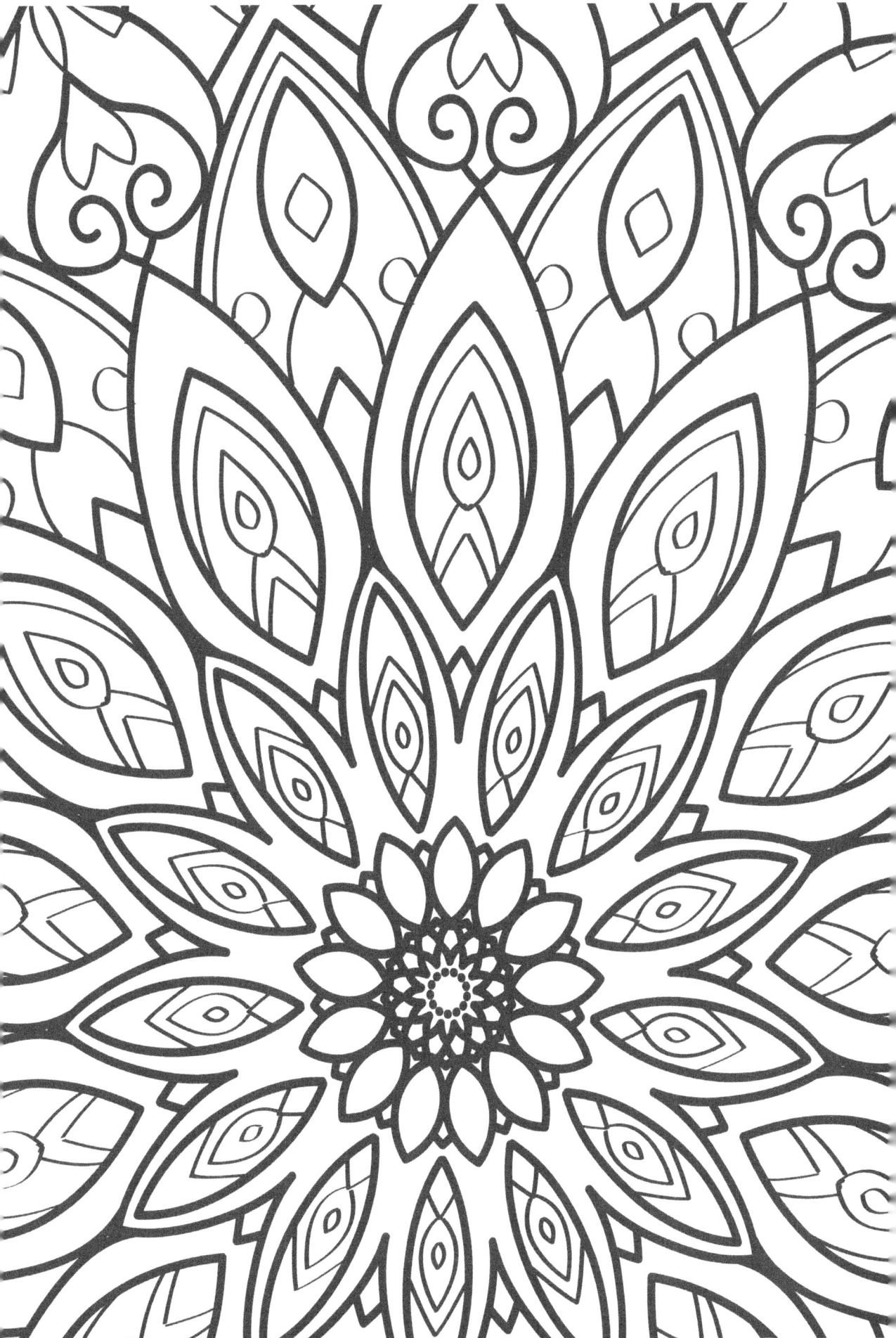

Coloring and drawing
are not tests,
not competition.

These are acts without
relative values.

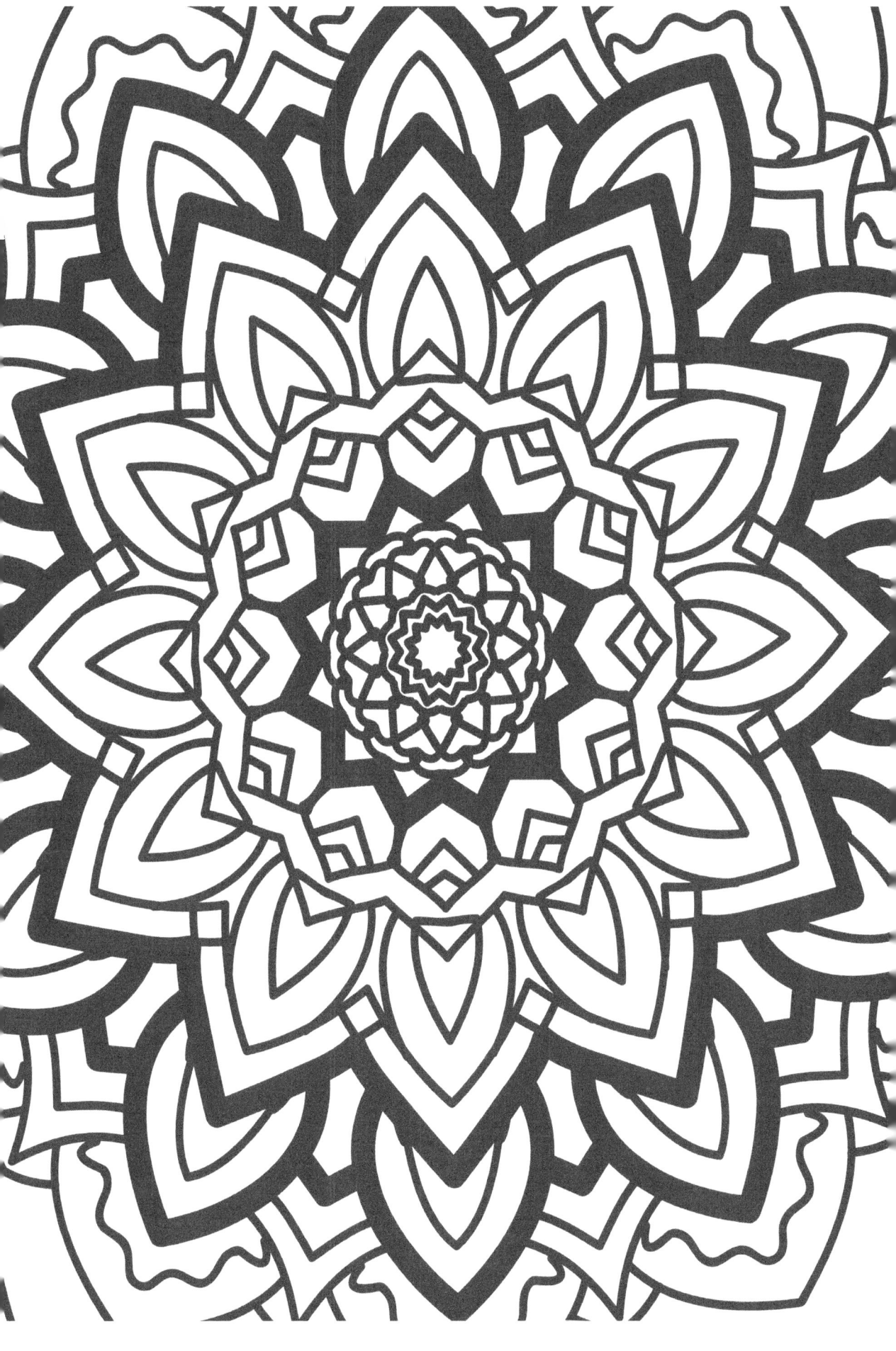

There's no outside

judge

to tell you you've done

well or poorly.

Just you, and the paper.

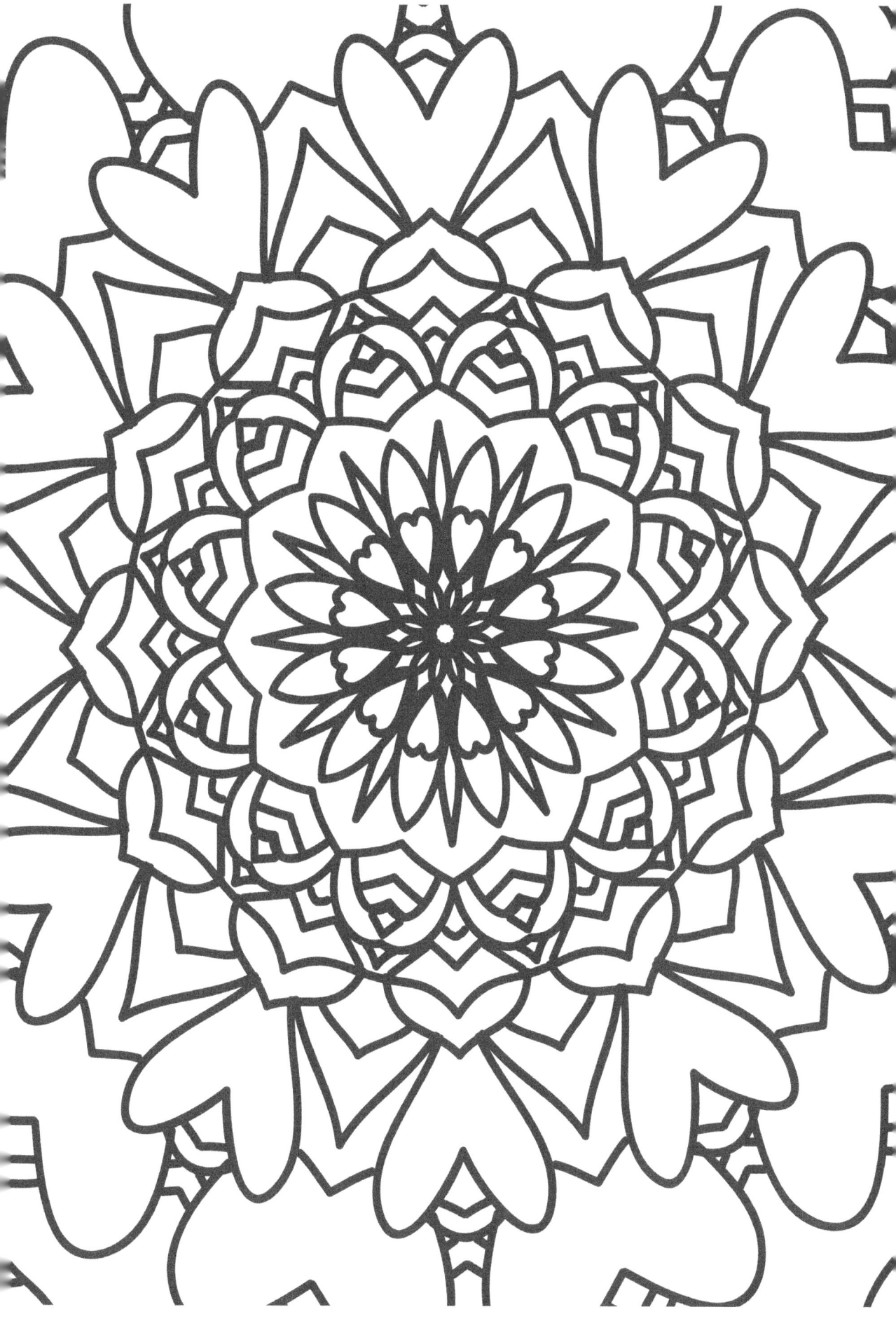

You can draw and color

without

any worry.

Just for fun.

Just for you.

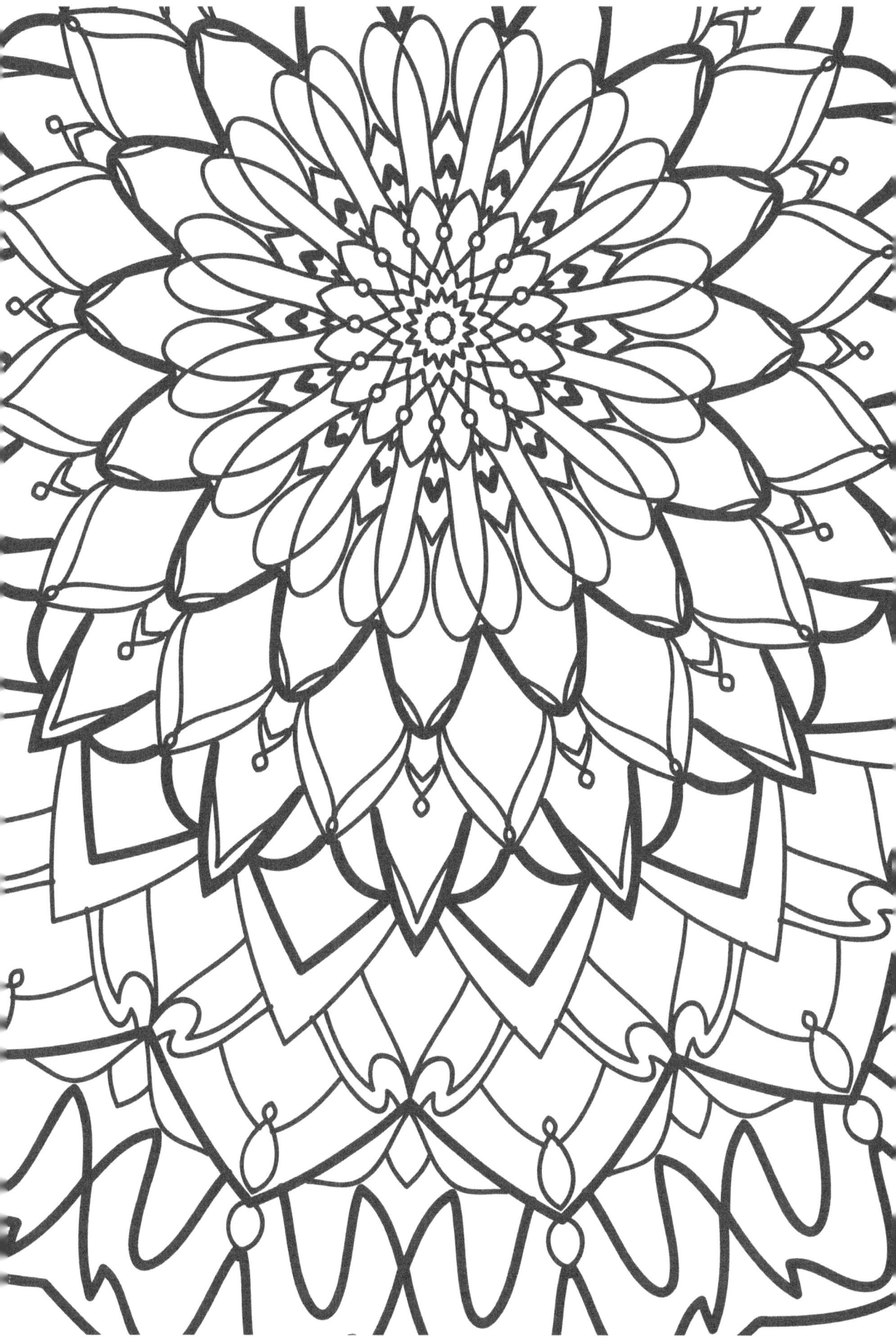

The way you draw,
the way you choose colors
and use them,
these are things that
are expressive.
They are part of
who you are.

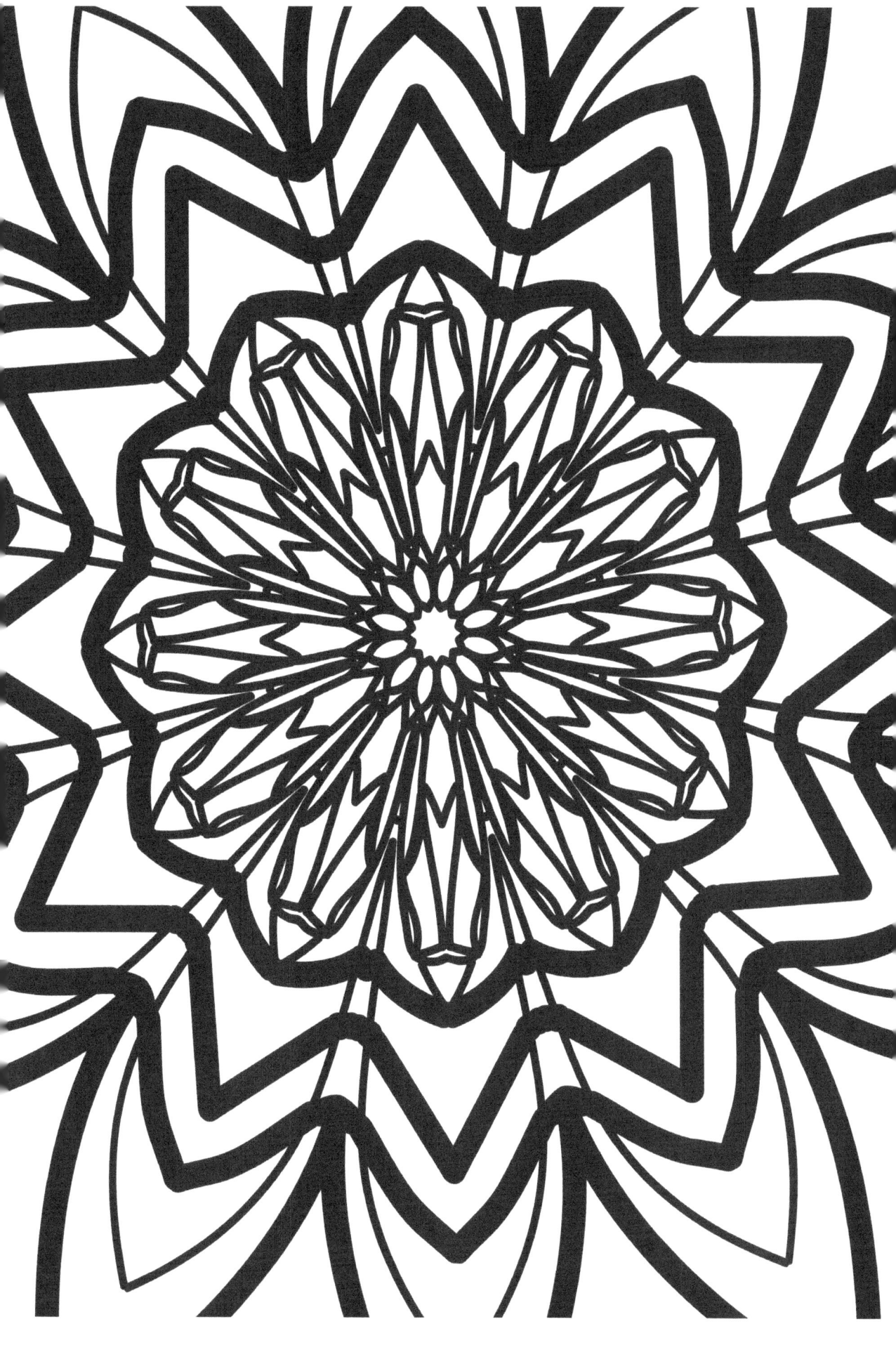

A favorite color combination

is a unique thing,

like the whorl of your hair

or fingerprint.

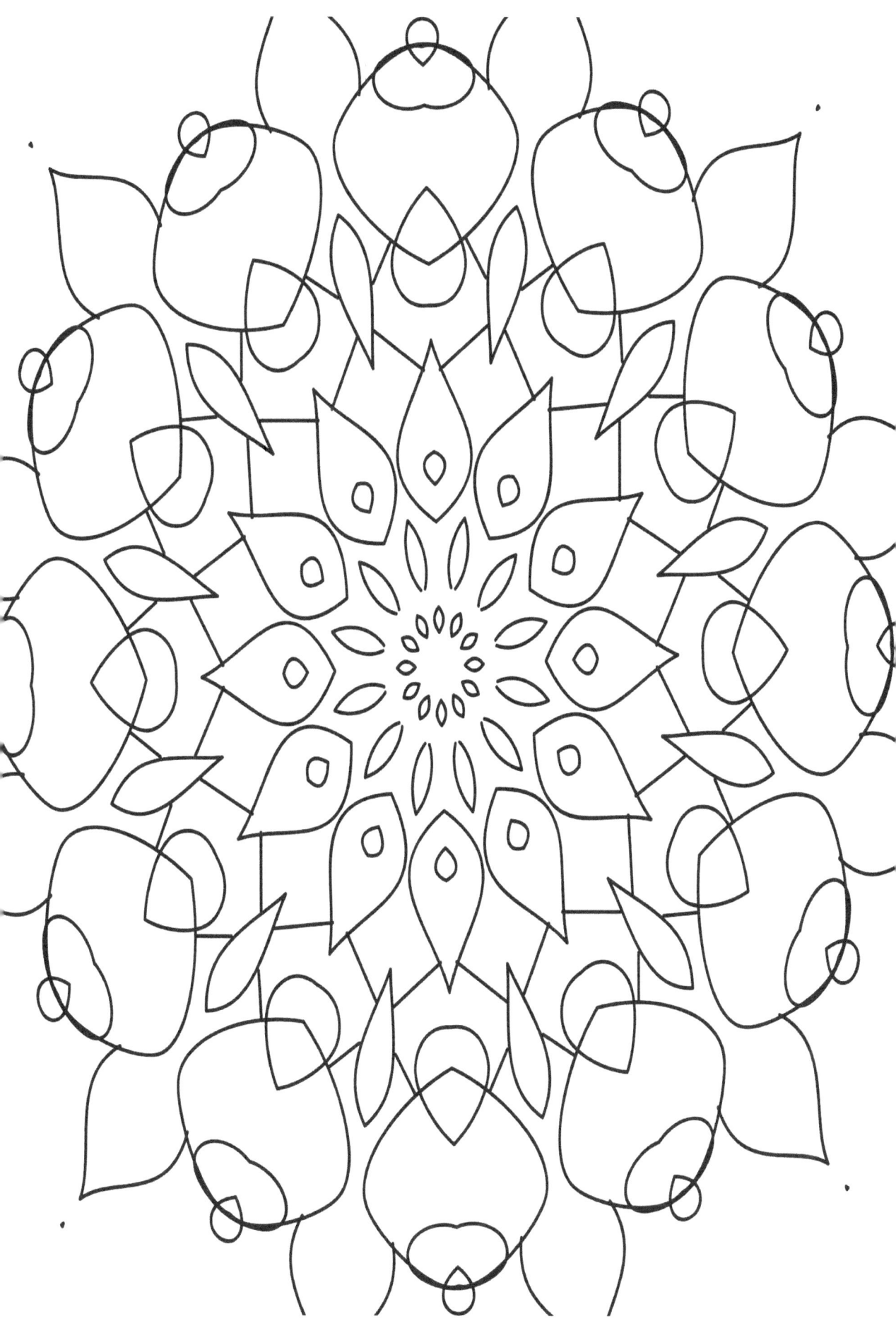

section two:

freestanding mandalas

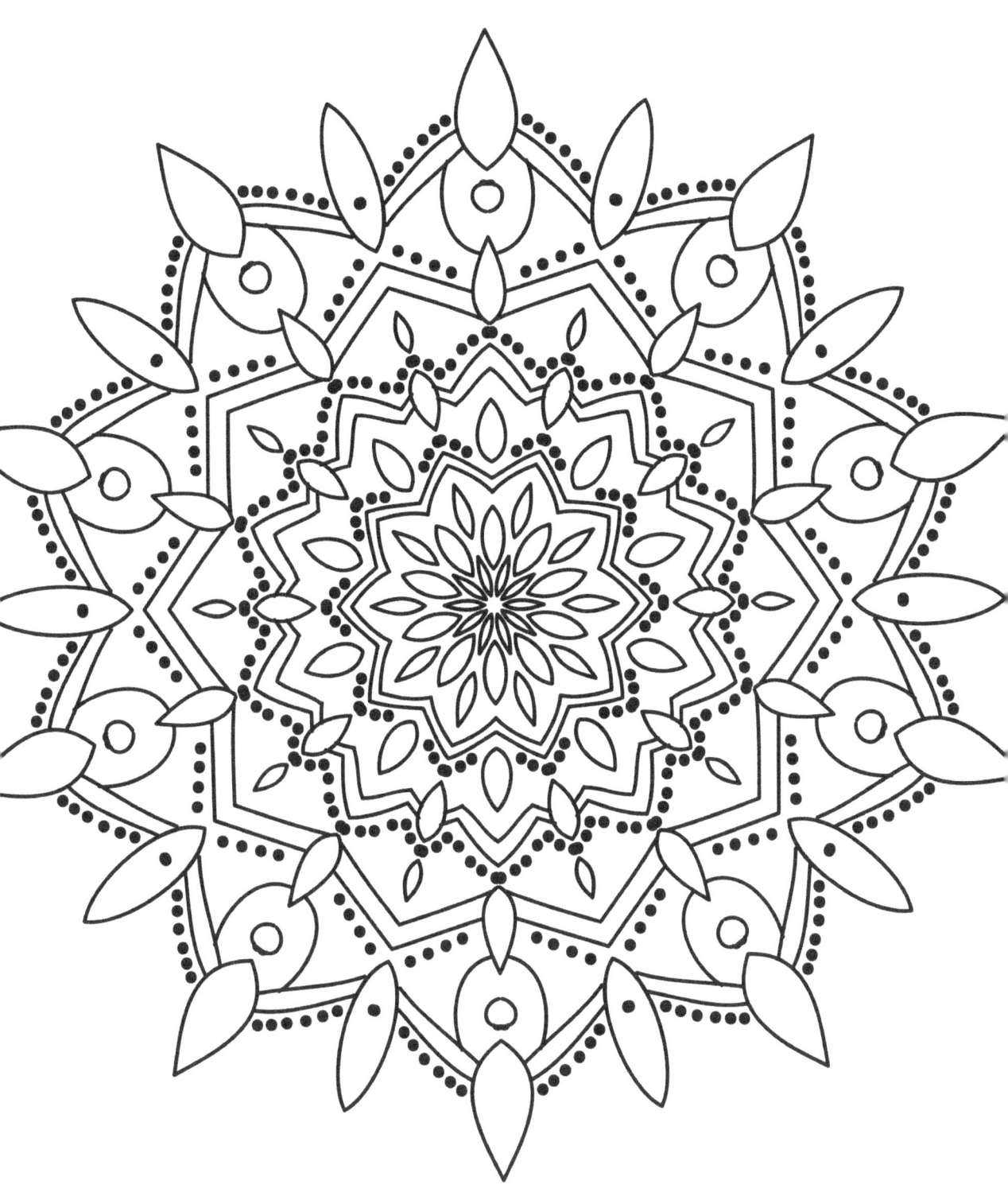

When you draw or color,

only you

could have done it

just that way.

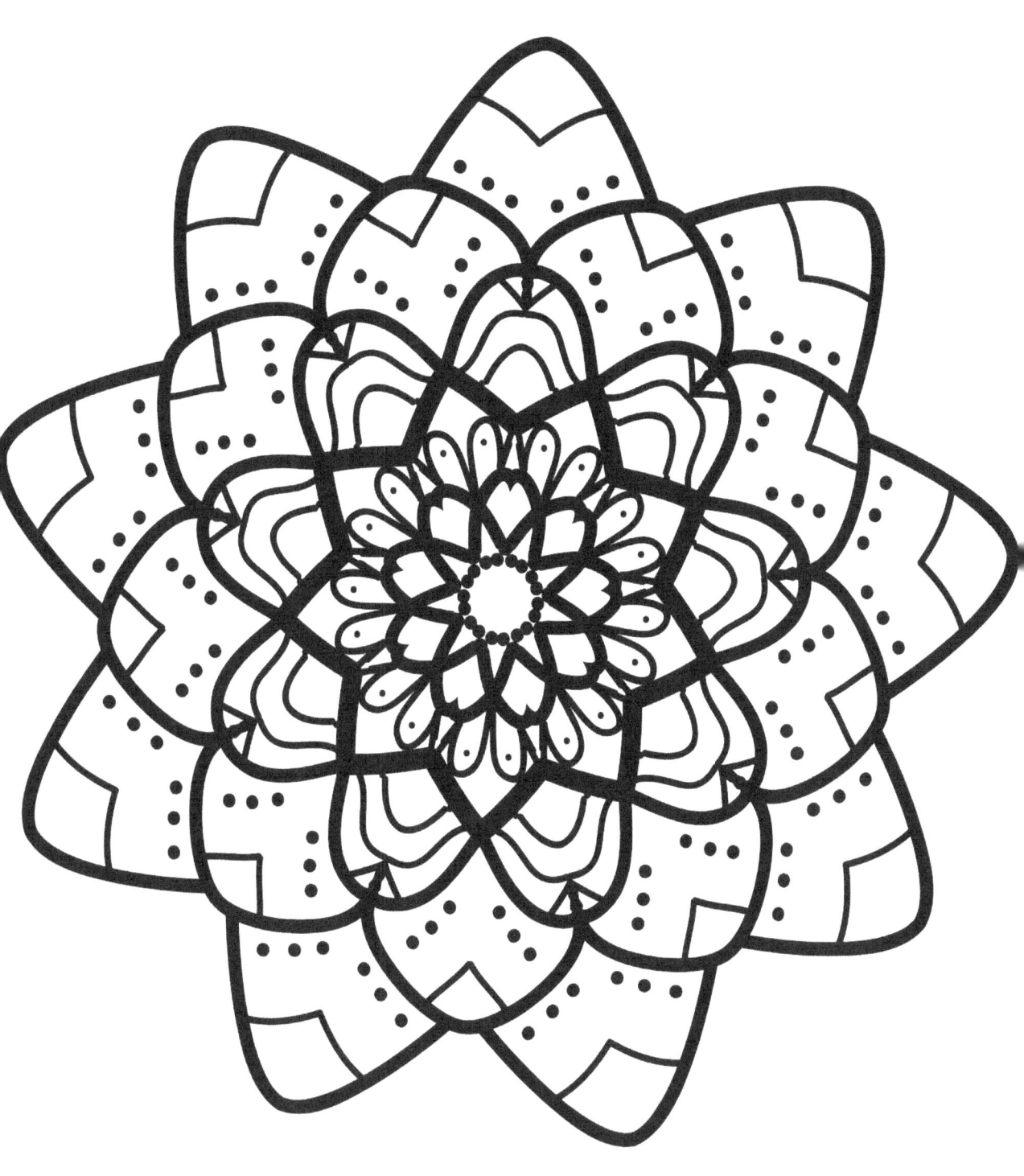

Anything you think

is a mistake

is just a bit of

hidden self

peeking out.

There's nothing wrong with that. There's nothing wrong with the way you draw or color.

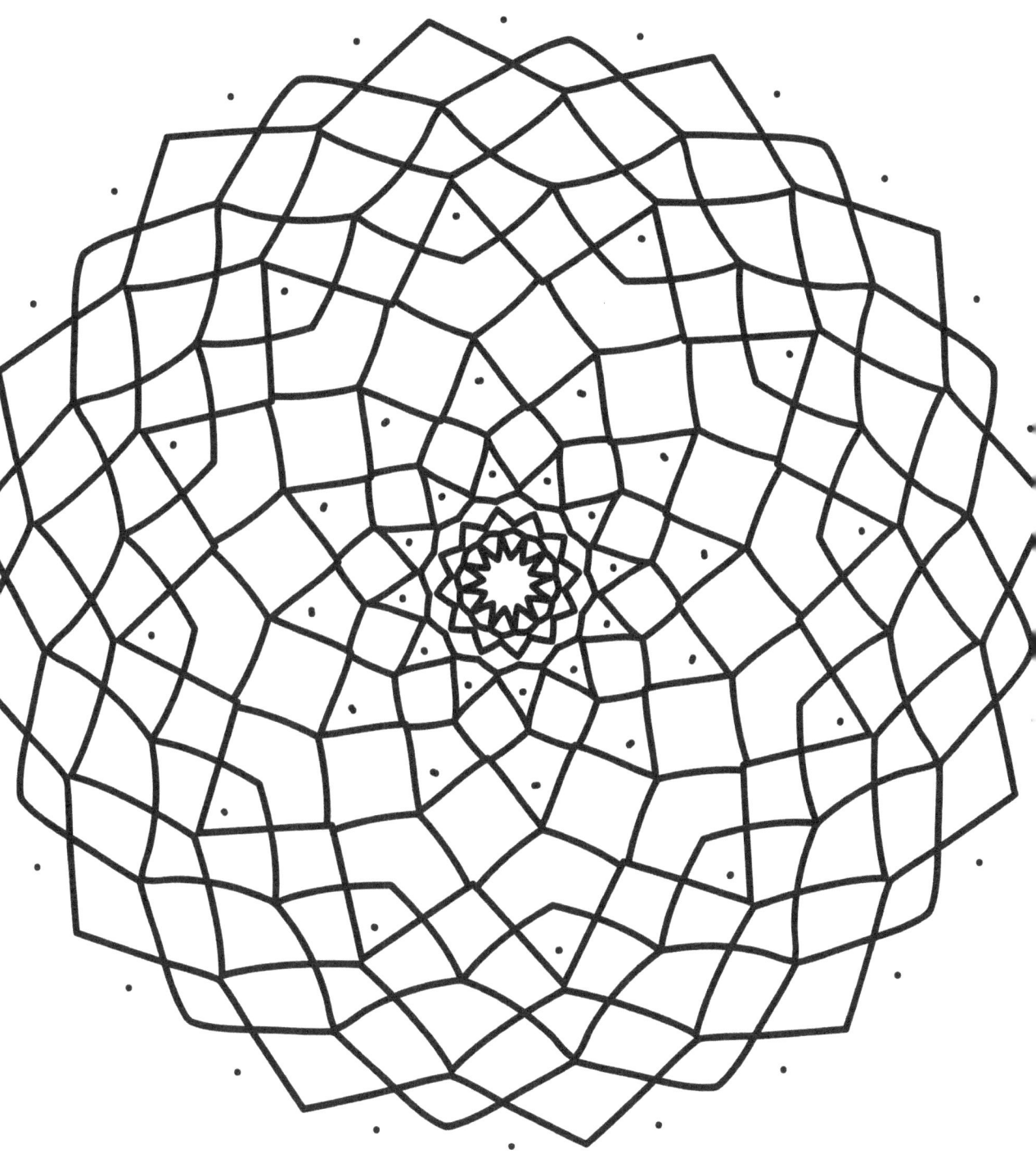

You can do anything

on paper

if you try your best,

you have done

everything perfectly.

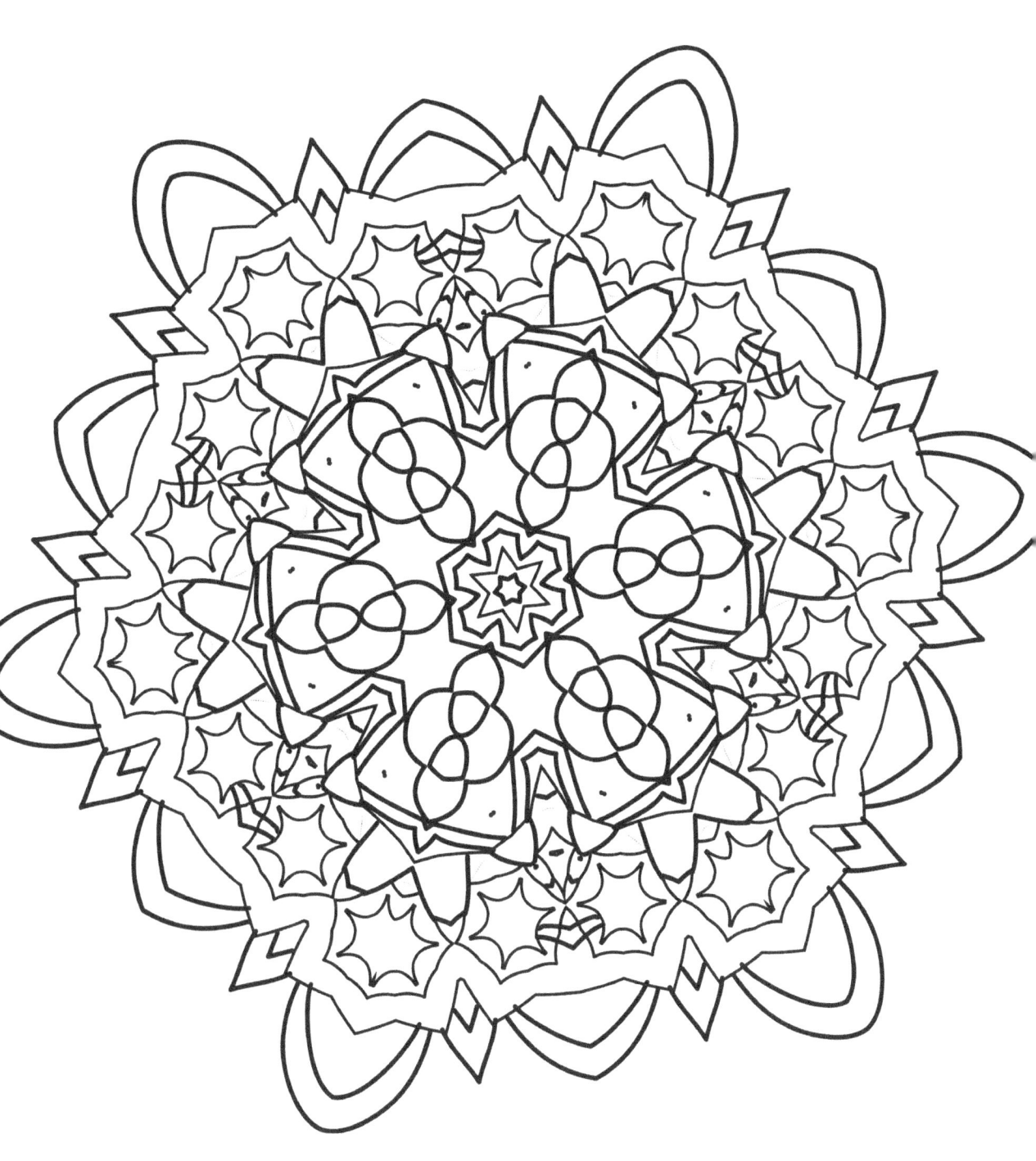

If you can't decide on colors or shapes, don't be afraid. There is a lot of paper in the world.

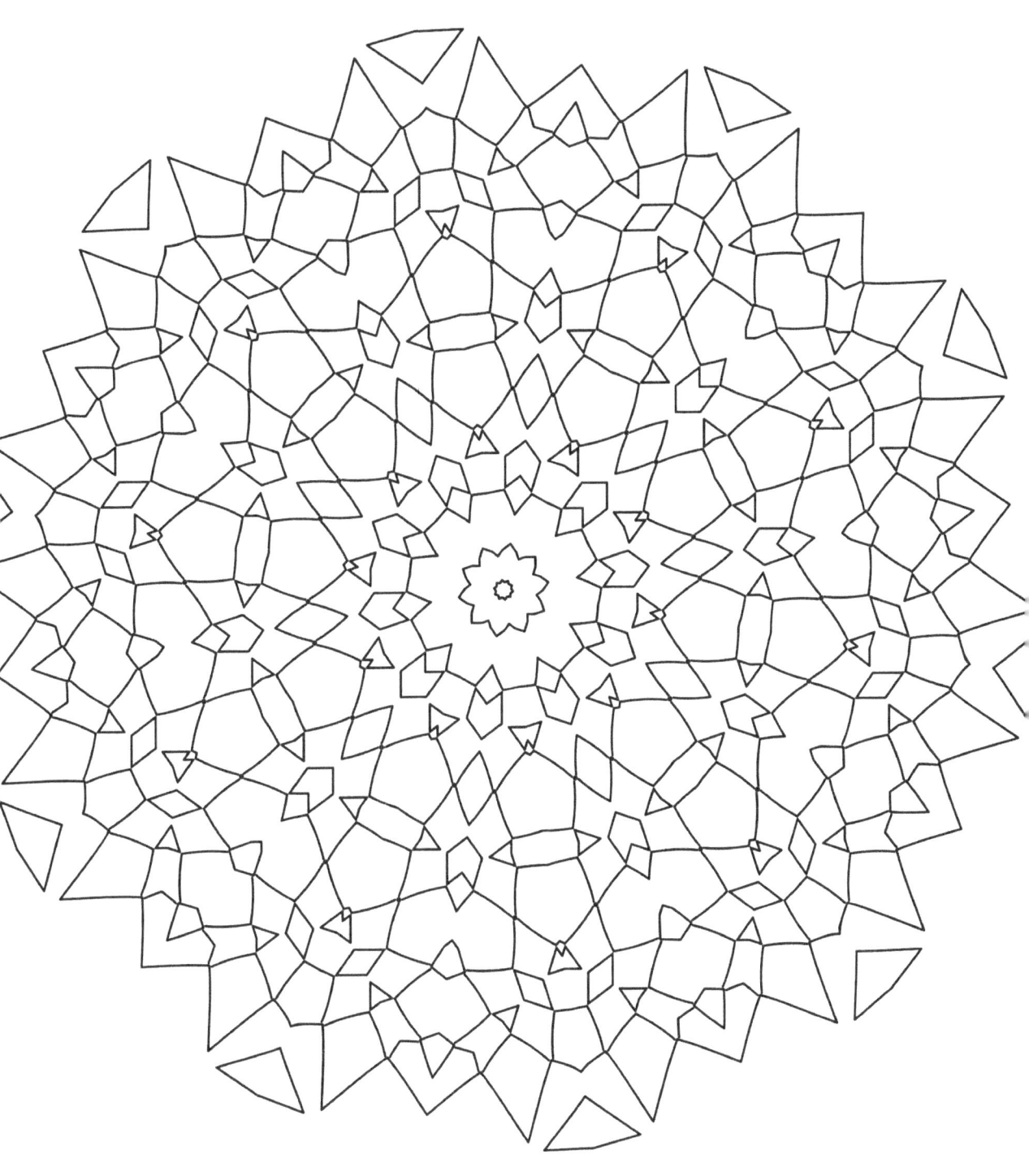

Even without paper,

there are walls,

there is chalk,

coal, dirt.

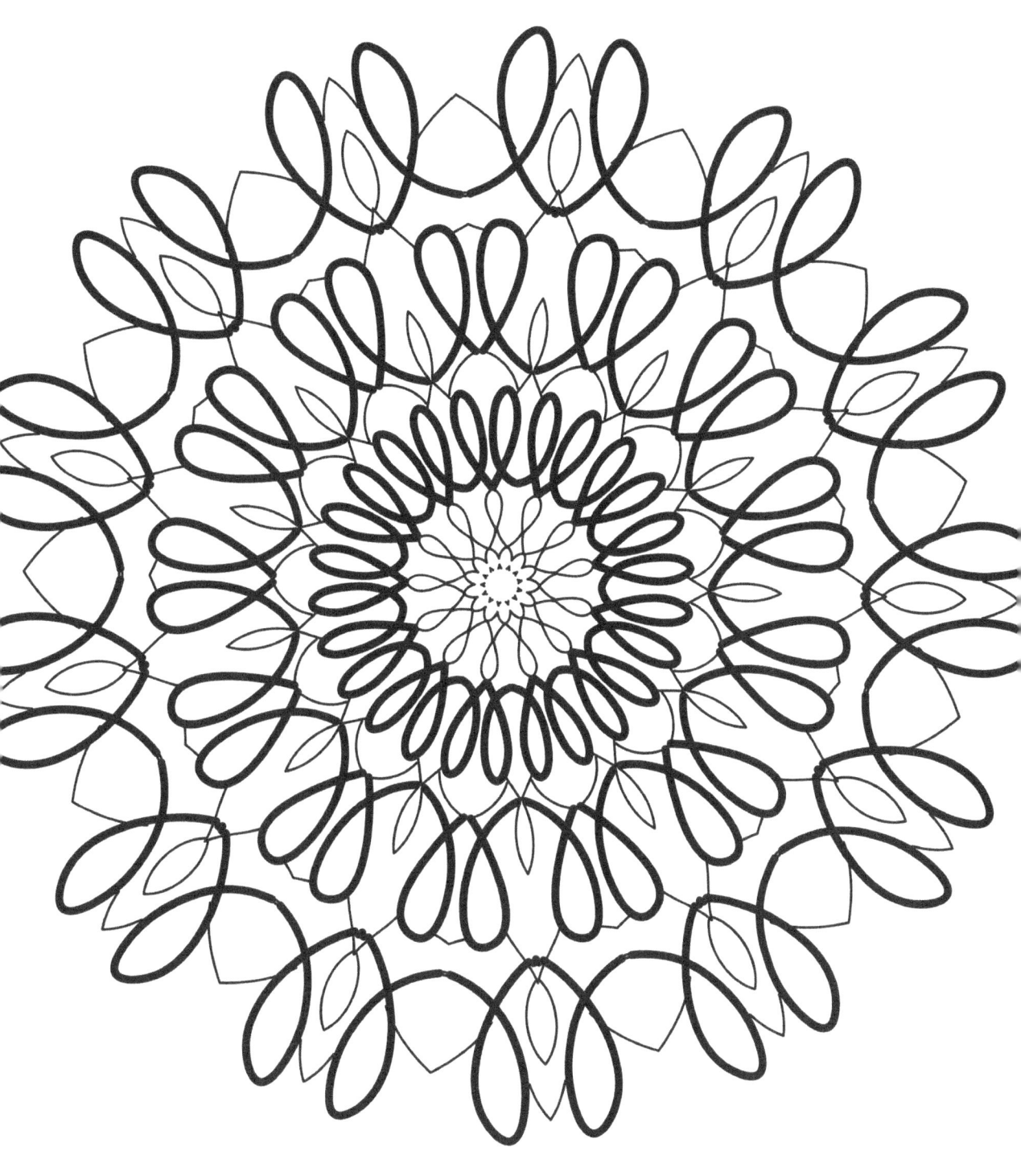

You can color with anything.

You can color on anything.

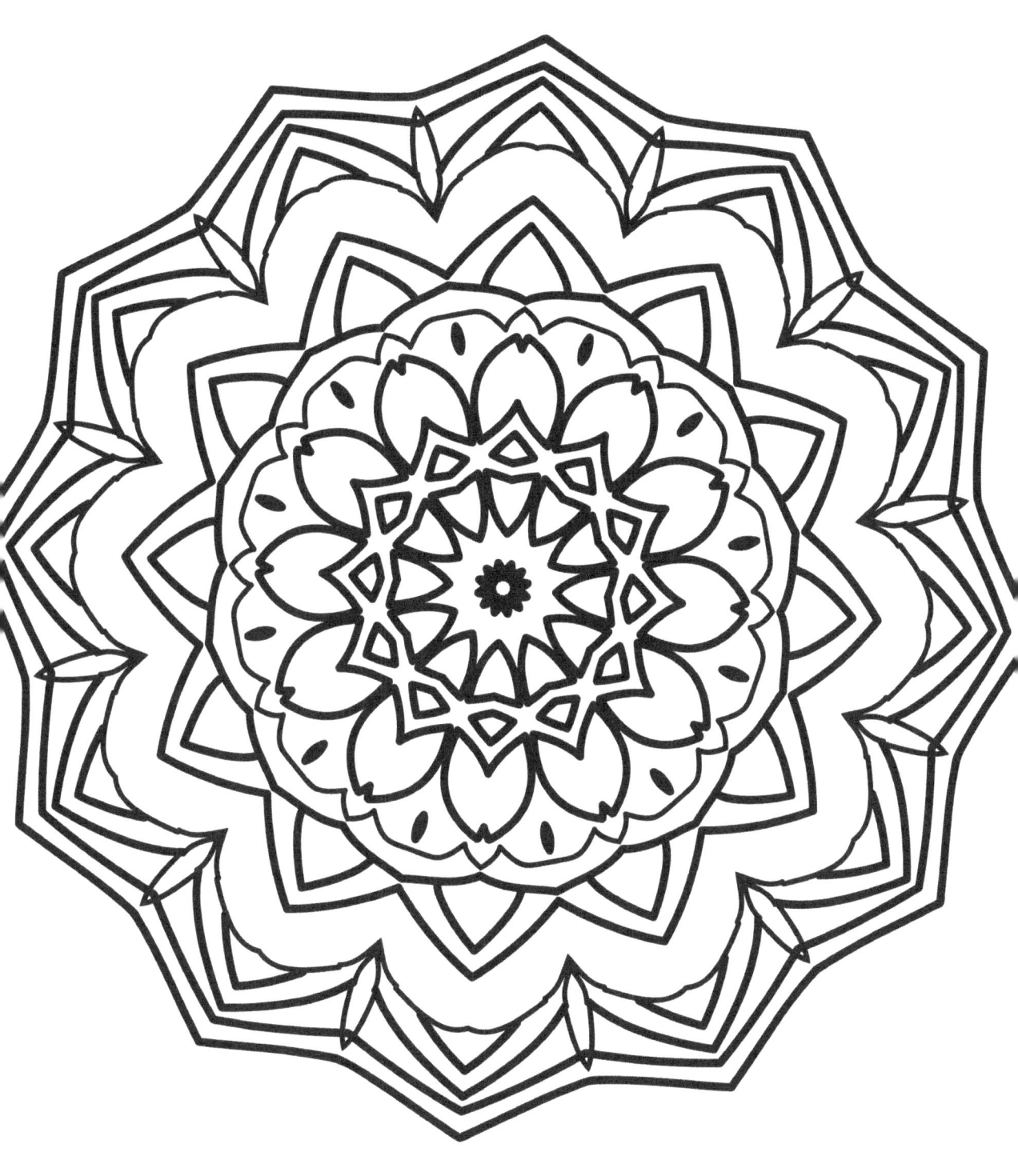

Drawing
and coloring things in

is a way to

make yourself

a part of the world.

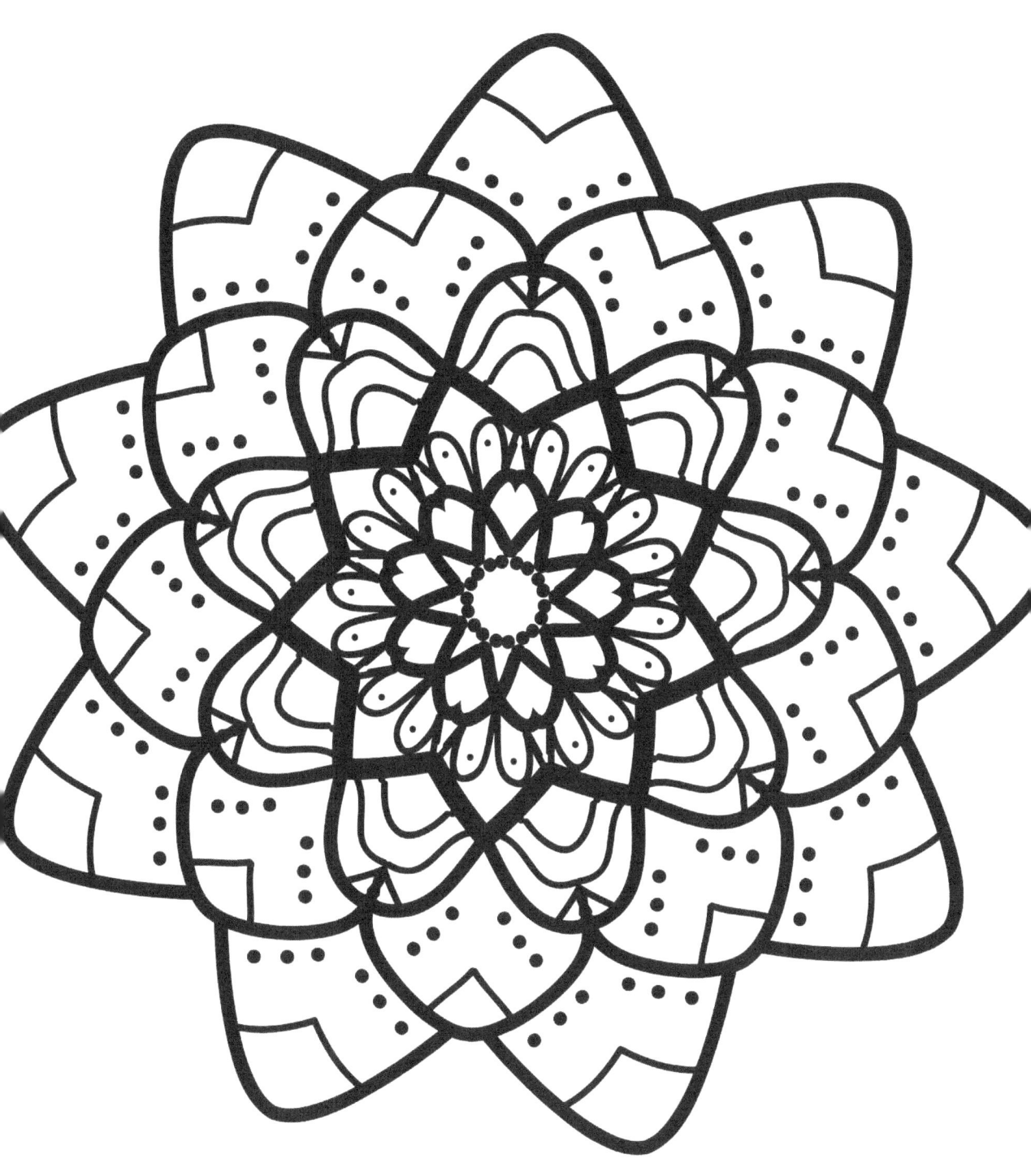

section three:

multiple line weight and

complexity

You are part of the world.

The things you do

are part of it.

What you decide to do

is unique.

Like that whorl.

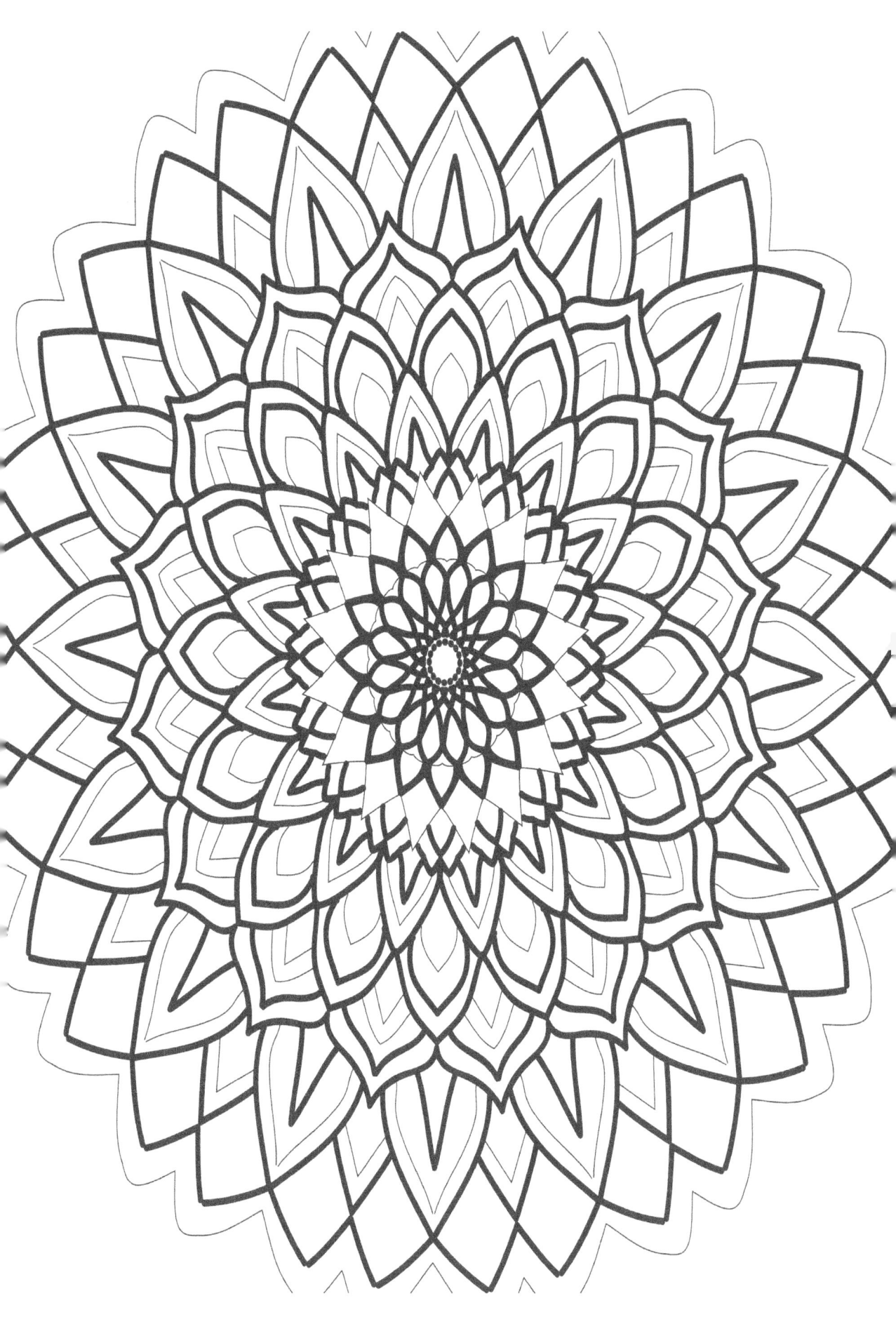

Every one of us

is a part of the world.

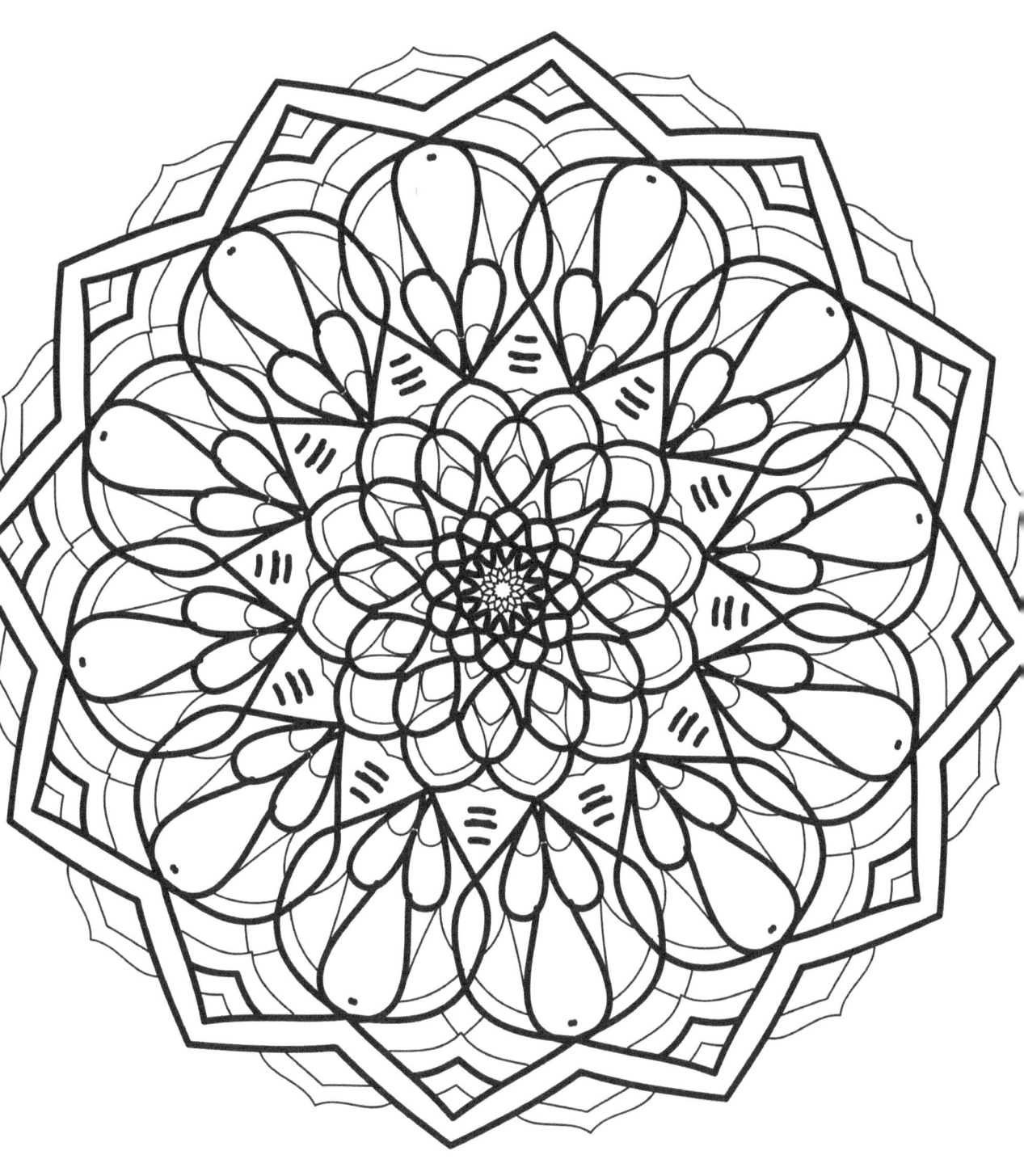

Every one of us is

important

to the world and

necessary to it.

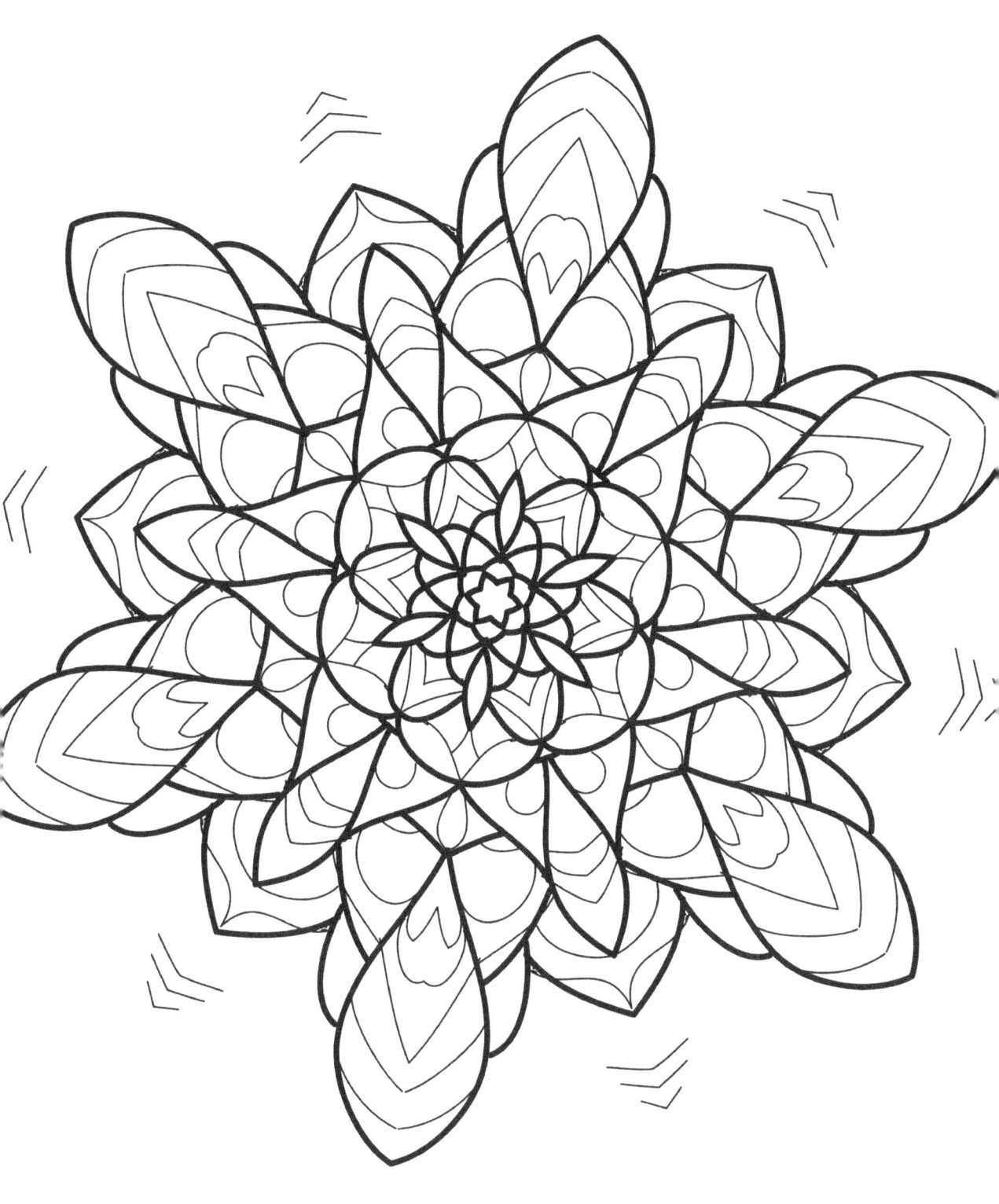

There is no reason
to be afraid of
coloring, of drawing.
There is no "wrong".

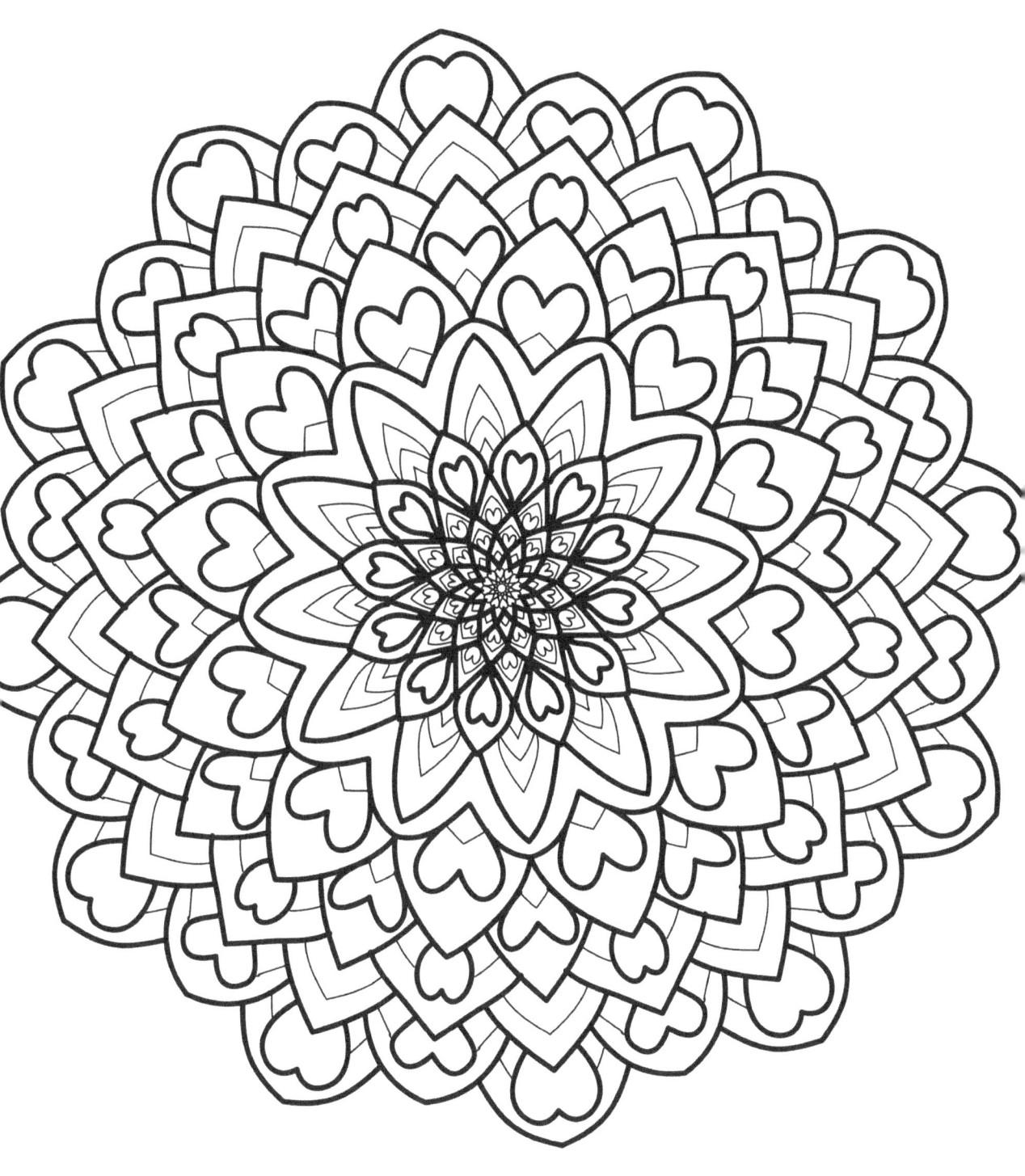

You can be

just who you are.

Doing your best

means you're doing

everything right.

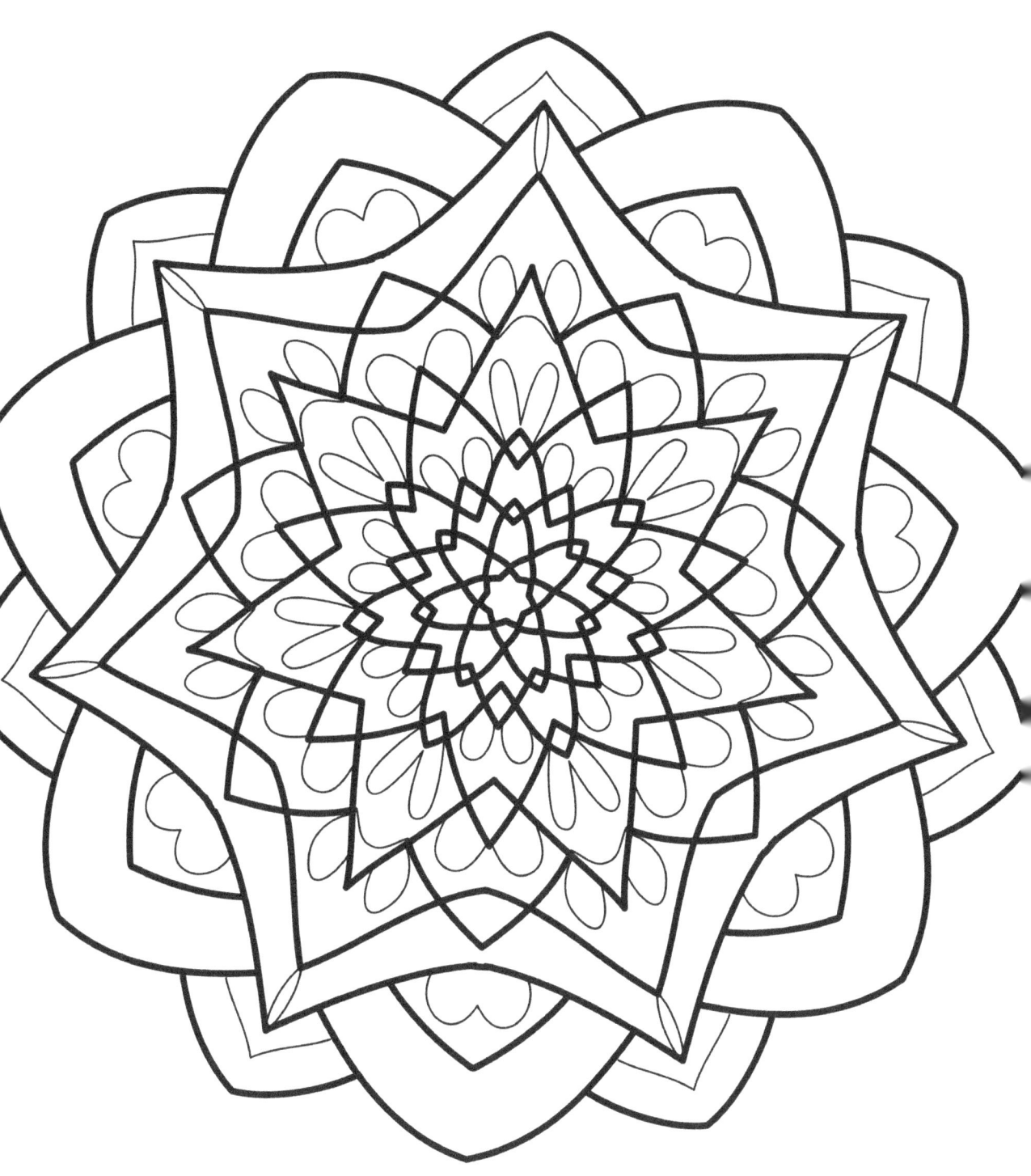

If you have a hard life,

do your best.

If you have an easy life,

do your best.

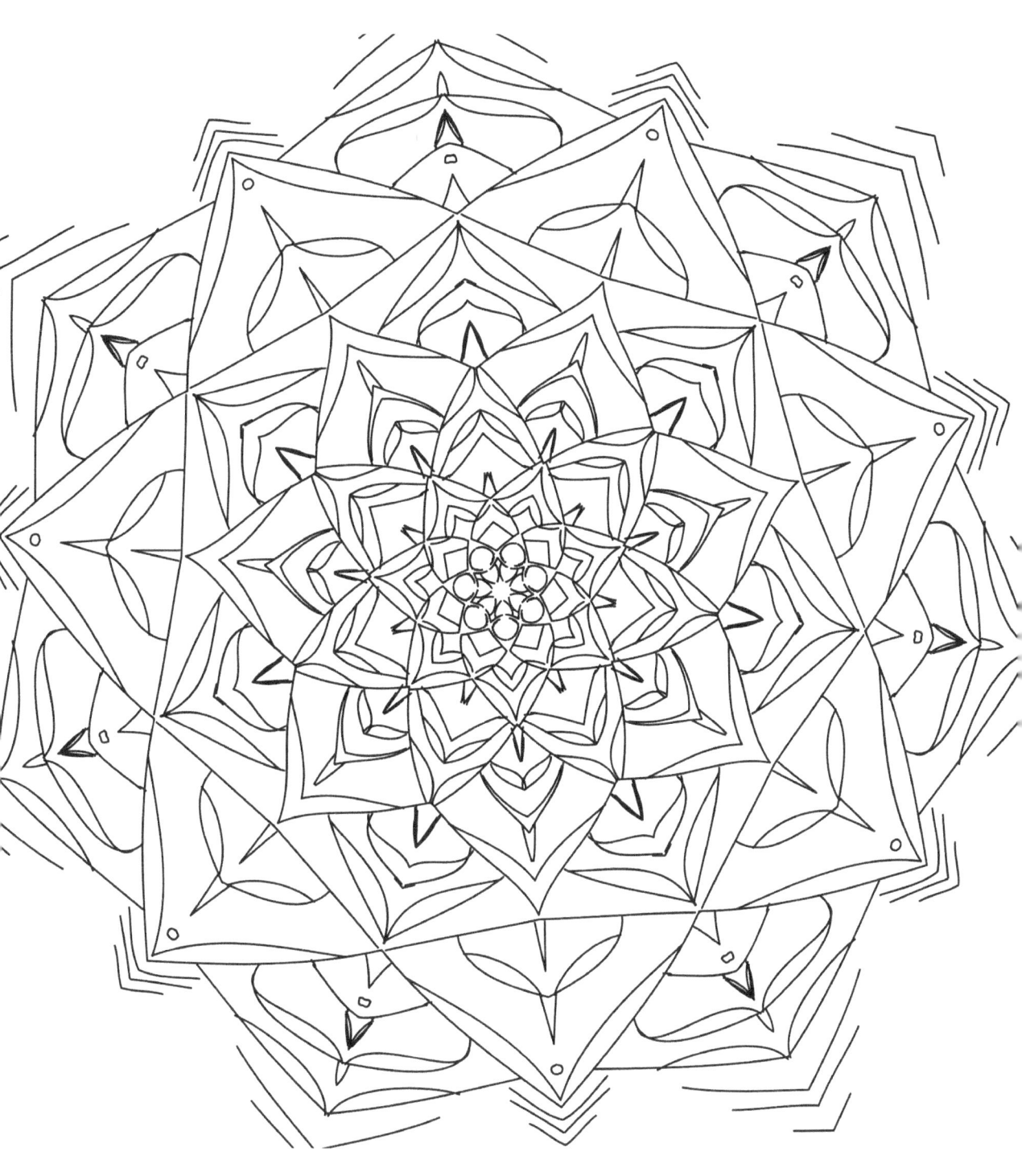

The mark you make
on the world
can only be made by you.
It is something
only you can do.

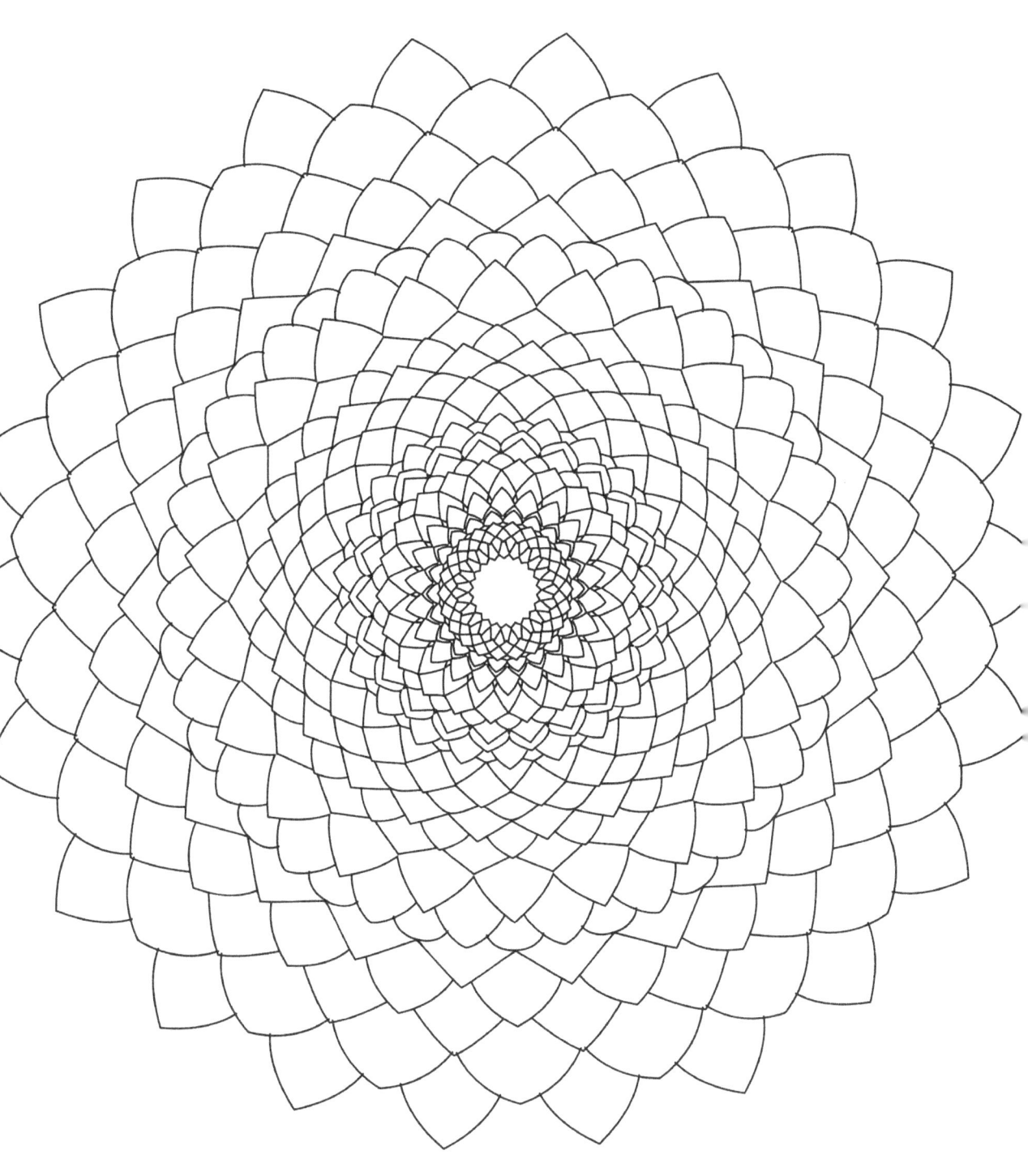

Nobody else
can do things just
exactly how you would.
We are all
different.

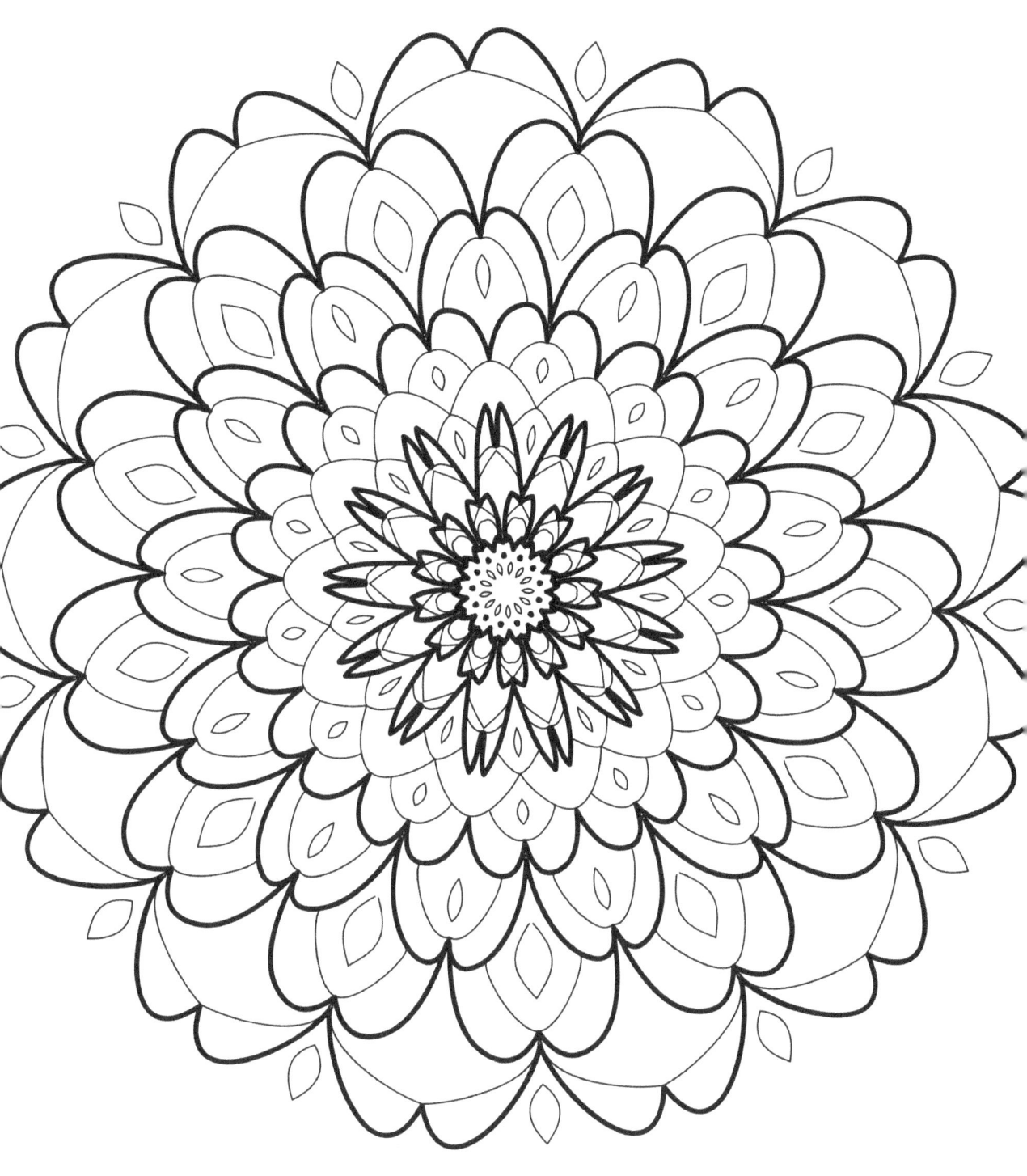

Other people's

marks

are visible if you look

for them.

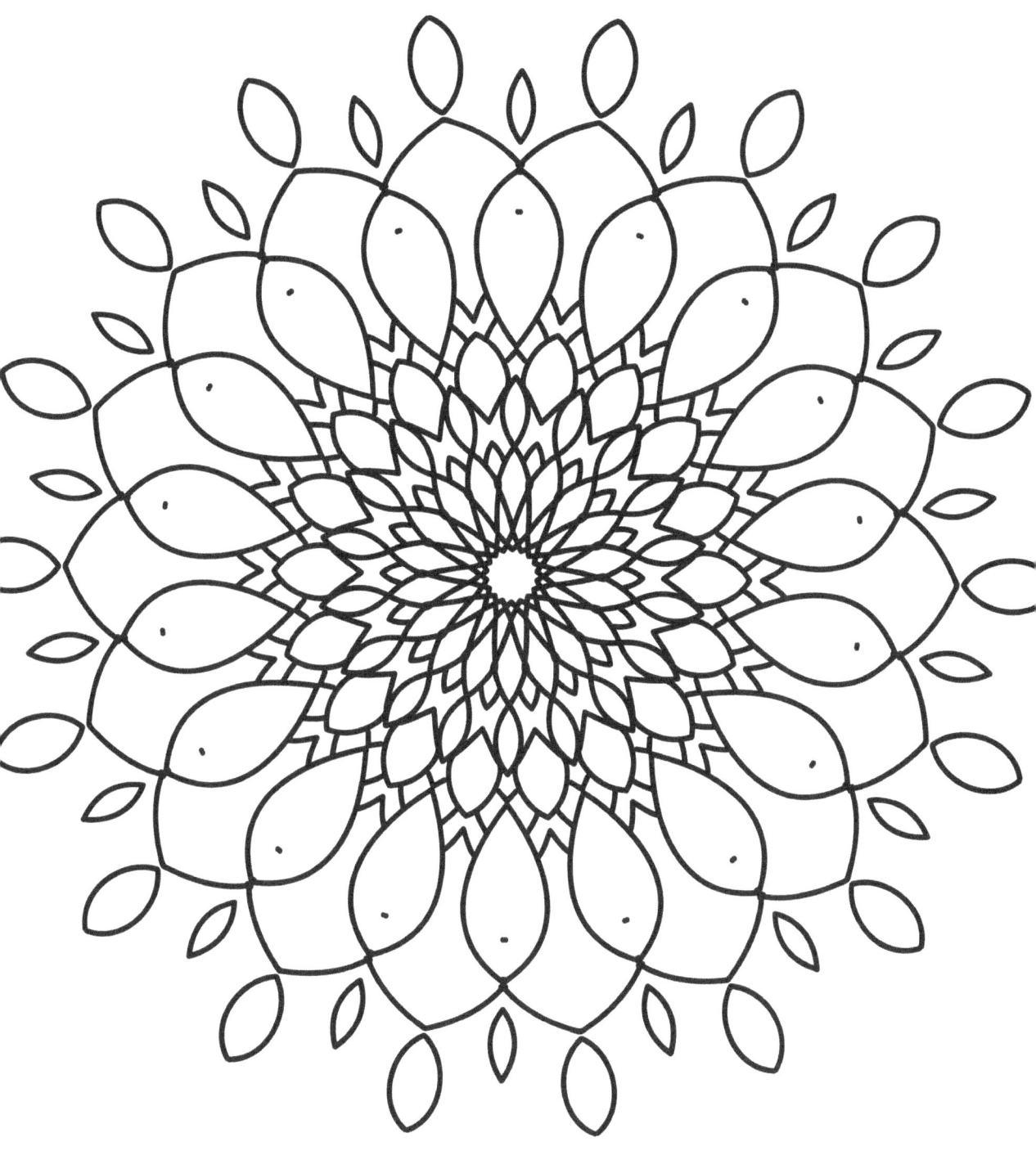

We are all

passing each other

notes,

all the time.

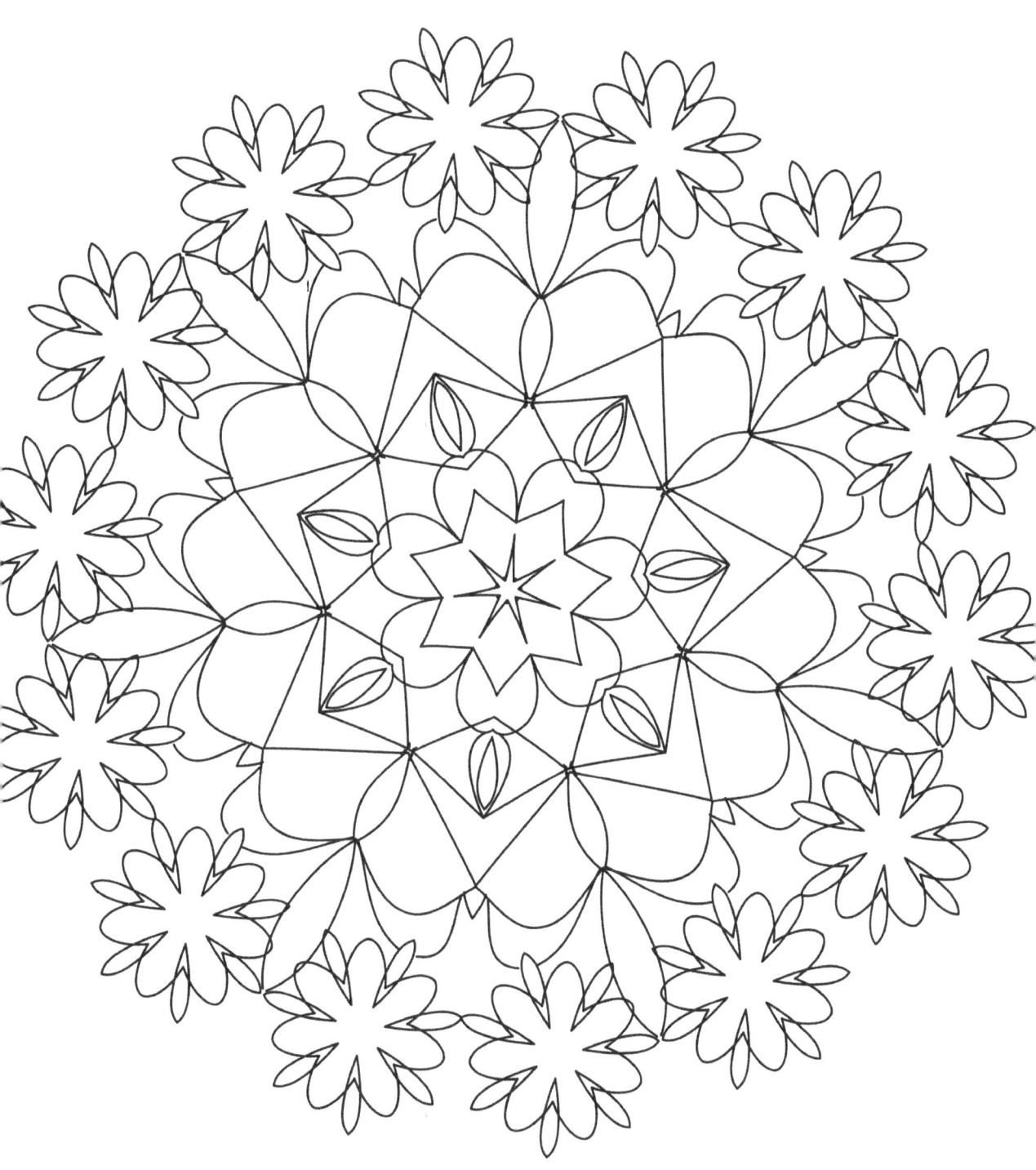

xox

find more at

resonanteye . net

www.ingramcontent.com/pod-product-compliance
Lightning Source LLC
Chambersburg PA
CBHW080647180526

45168CB00008B/3329